How To Win In Tennis Leagues

Dedicated to my tennis loving family, and all those for whom games are still just play.

How To Win In Tennis Leagues

Copyright 2007 by Samuel W. Hopkins, Jr., Ph.D.

ISBN 978-0-9802247-0-2
Library of Congress 2007910130
First Edition 2007

Published by the SamPat Press
Printed in the United States of America
by Lightning Source, Inc.

Design and layout by Christine D. Kjosa

Edited by Donald R. Doggett
and Betty Marcontell

Correspondence and publication requests contact:
SamPat Press
1027 Timothy, Jacksonville, Texas 75766
(903) 586-4488
http://sampatpress.com/

Table of Contents

Preface

You may have noticed that some tennis teams win league titles year after year, even while changing playing rosters. You, too, can have a perennial winner by using a few sound principles that some of us have learned to employ. Forming, managing, and playing on a championship tennis team requires special skills and knowledge. If you are going to construct such a team and be a leading player on the roster, you will need more than just a good personality and a great first serve. Here's some practical advice about how to do it.

For openers, you need not be the best player in the lineup to be the leading contributor to the success of a winning team. For instance, my teams have learned that it might be better if the team captain is **not** the strongest person on the roster (see Chapter 2 about why this is true). Such strategic insights are the kind of lessons many of us wish we had learned before we ever formed our first team. If only I could have read a handbook about **How To Win In Team Leagues**, it would have been a lot easier to prepare for competition.

Since there was no such training manual in 2000 when our first team was organized, I compared notes and talked shop with other players and teams about what we were supposed to be doing. Thus, in our limited circles, talking a good game became as important as playing a good game. After receiving several requests to share our court wisdom with other teams, some of my teammates suggested that this information should be published for the benefit of others. Most of the team captains and sophisticated players with whom I have consulted were amateur players in our favorite lifetime sport. This collective wisdom has come from "on the job" experience, and from our losses as much as victories. Early on you learn that success requires more than merely registering a team roster, having a team practice, and making a lineup for your matches.

Please note: you do not have to be a team captain to appreciate and benefit from the court experience compiled in this text. If you think like a captain when you play your matches, you will be much more valuable to your team on and off the court. One of my first USTA sectional championship teams, a 6.0 senior mixed doubles roster, was completely composed of players who had served as team captains at one time or another. They were the easiest group to manage of any team thus far because they understood and appreciated the tactical arrangements that brought them success. This book is dedicated to all such thinking people who play league tennis.

Sometimes the lessons learned seem like only common sense solutions to personnel management and playing situations. Well, maybe so, but this knowledge wasn't always so obvious before we organized our teams. Furthermore, with added experience our initial insights have been revised from time to time (logically implying that a second edition of this handbook will have to be published someday). One corollary about winning is that there will always be more to learn about playing competitive tennis. We have to keep improving our strategies since the competition keeps getting better and better, and there are always more titles to be won.

Once you have used the lessons of **How To Win In Team Leagues**, your teams can certainly be as good as mine, or maybe better. Your victories may very well stimulate my teams to find better ways to win their matches. If so, we will thank you for pushing us to perform at even higher levels of competition. Your achievements might even become material for an advanced sequel about winning in tennis leagues. For sure, your successes will certainly delight my publisher, since your championships will serve as a good testimonial about the value of using this handbook. So here's to your team and mine. May we play each other every year in the finals of the state and national championships.

Sam Hopkins
Jacksonville (TX) Tennis Hall of Fame 2003
Texas Section USTA Community Service Award 2005
USTA Eve Kraft Community Service Award 2005

Chapter 1

FROM ZERO TO THE TRIPLE CROWN

Winning in tennis leagues means going from having no hometown 3.0 men's teams in 1999 in our local tennis league to becoming the first team in the first 25 years of USTA league history ever to win the "triple crown" of sectional competition in 2005. In that remarkable year, the Jacksonville men's team won the Texas sectional titles for the 3.0 adult men, 3.0 senior men (age 50 and older), and 6.0 super senior men's (age 60 and older) tennis leagues. Up until that time no team of men or women of any rating level in America had ever swept all three age groups in sectional championships at the same time.

Winning in tennis leagues means having 16 of my small town 3.0 men and 6.0 mixed doubles teams qualify and participate in the USTA Texas sectional championships and USPTA state championships since 2002. In this millennium, these teams have won five state titles, and finished as the state runner-up six times. Our teams come from a small East Texas town of 14,000 people, and compete in a wide spread geographical area with teams from larger cities of up to 80,000 population. When our teams advance from our Northeast Texas District league to the state playoffs, we play the champions from the multi-million population centers of Houston, Dallas, and San Antonio. Our small town team delights in playing the role of little David in slaying these teams of giant Goliaths.

Winning in tennis leagues means having players from these various championship teams promoted to higher playing levels and winning league titles in these leagues, too. In 2004, the Jacksonville men's teams simultaneously swept the Northeast Texas championships in three levels of USTA competition (3.0, 3.5 and 4.0 men), thereby winning our area's triple crown of men's team tennis. In a short, five-year period our town had developed a preeminent tennis culture and tradition of winning in leagues. Because of these and other local accomplishments, the Jacksonville Tennis Association (which I founded in 1977) received the best mid-sized Community Tennis Association award in 2004 from the Texas Section USTA. Our record is a source of civic pride, and has primarily come from the community's enthusiastic participation in tennis leagues.

These tennis league successes occurred because we learned and practiced some important lessons about winning through good team management. In a very short period of competition, our town went from having no teams in my playing category to winning it all. These lessons have come from widespread experience in personally organizing and managing teams in every age category and both genders in USTA, USPTA, and WTT leagues. The principles of winning in tennis leagues are always the same. Knowing them is a start. Using them takes practice. Talent helps, too.

TENNIS IS A TEAM SPORT NOW

Tennis competition has increasingly become a team sport - the best thing to happen in recreational tennis since the introduction of the yellow ball and the graphite racquet. Team play fundamentally changes the perspective and preparation for matches. Except for the Davis Cup and Federation Cup formats, traditional tennis has been about individual playing records in elimination style tournaments. The popular image of tennis competition is the singles finals of a grand slam event like the All England Lawn Tennis Championships on the quick grassy courts of Wimbledon stadium in London. The hard charging, racquet-swinging combatants struggling with each other on center court epitomize the sport in the public's mind. To this day, the largest prize money still goes to the single's champions in a professional tennis tournament.

Playing by yourself can be highly rewarding, and is simpler to manage. Team play can be very equally satisfying, but is a more complex operation. Others are affected by your victories or defeats, and vice versa. Team management requires communication, coordination, and collaboration for the good of the whole. **The foremost principle of winning in tennis leagues is banding together for victory.** Teams are about being "all for one, and one for all." The rallying cry must be about brotherhood and sisterhood on the courts. Sharing and caring is absolutely essential for success in a team sport. Loners need not apply.

John McEnroe's advocacy of playing on the USA Davis Cup tennis team has been an inspiring example of motivating players to unite in a common cause. His social consciousness and inspirational cohesiveness have made him as famous for his outstanding doubles record as for his sensational singles achievements. The players on your team must have this attitude about winning, and it's up to the team leadership to instill such esprit de corps in the roster.

Granted that fellowship is a key motivator and benefit of playing on tennis teams, the league-playing format is a big attraction, too. The round-robin team-playing schedule used in leagues allows all participants to play the same number of matches, win or lose. The worst part of traditional tournament competition is that after the first round of play, half of the entrants are "one and done," unless there is a consolation bracket. Even then, many contestants will only get to play twice. Most tournament tennis uses a player elimination format that rewards winners with continued play. Losers are left out, even though they are the very people who most need more opportunities to practice their skills. You have to play in matches in order to improve your game. Tennis leagues keep everybody in the game until the end of a well-defined schedule of matches.

A fixed schedule of matches set up on a regular basis for league play is, in itself, an extra benefit of tennis team competition. Typically, a team plays once a week over an extended length of time. League style play has a cumulative beneficial effect on a player's concentration and playing intensity. The team must get ready for competition every week. Team players have strong incentives to practice regularly for their many important matches. Over time these preparations increase playing competency on and off the courts. Continuous competition sharpens a player's game. Tennis leagues keep us well focused, something that is hard to maintain when entering occasional tournaments. If practice makes perfect, tennis teams are a good way to get better.

Another virtue of tennis team league competition is the round robin format. Everybody plays each other in the schedule of league matches. You get to play a variety of opponents, from the very best ones to the last place finishers. You will have easy matches to build your confidence, and there will be challenging contests that will make you work harder on all parts of your game. By playing against the full range of opponents in a league, we have a way to estimate our relative standing in tennis, and can measure our personal progress in the sport. To the everlasting credit of tennis league competition, there is no "seeding" of teams according to abilities in a round-robin schedule. In traditional tournaments with player elimination formats, the strong are protected from each other initially at the expense of lesser opponents; how very unfair, and a good reason to prefer the egalitarian league schedules such as team tennis employs. Round robin schedules help reduce the luck of the draw phenomenon so prevalent in elimination style tournaments.

ALL ABOUT LEAGUES

Winning in tennis team leagues begins with knowing how to find a program where you can compete for titles. The most common questions about winning a tennis league are how to enter a team, and what are the rules and formats of the competition. Many league players lack even basic information about what they will be doing or how it has been arranged, except for word of mouth sources in limited circles. Becoming well informed about league programs is vitally important for every team member; especially for people who assume responsibility for managing a team, particularly if it's for the very first time.

Finding out about a league and its operation can be critically important to your team's survival, much less success. For instance, in USTA leagues, a team can be disqualified for a whole season if they fail to show up for a scheduled match. One team captain did not have a full lineup to travel for an out-of-town match and decided to forfeit the contest; only to learn afterwards that his team could not play the rest of their schedule because of league rules that require teams to play every match or be eliminated. This sad, disappointing case demonstrates how important it is to know what's going on and where to find the information you need. You can get connected with local league playing networks by calling the nearest community tennis association, or contacting the nearest teaching tennis pro, or by using the web sites on the internet for the major established league programs. There are enough league programs operating to let you play year round if you know how to find them and how to use them.

The three best providers and organizers of tennis team league programs are the USTA, the USPTA, and the WTT. If you know what these leagues have to offer, you can win a room full of trophies and titles.

United States Tennis Association (USTA) Leagues:

www.usta.com

The United States Tennis Association has, by far, the largest and most prestigious nationwide league program, with the best online information network in American tennis. USTA sponsored league competition encompass over 550,000 players. Teams can progress from local leagues through state or sectional tournaments all the way to a national championship. The size and scope of USTA leagues insures that you will have many opportunities to win championships -- more than any other league program. Be prepared for strong competition. There are a lot of good tennis players in America; and if they play in tennis leagues, they are sure to be found in the USTA programs.

USTA leagues require that players have a current USTA membership that extends through the completion of the league schedule for their team. The fastest way to get an individual membership needed to play on a league team is to call the USTA toll free phone number at 1-800-990-8782. You will need to use a credit card to pay for your membership fee if you join over the phone. You can also join the USTA on the internet by using their website and your credit card. Or, you can use the old fashion postal mailing method of mailing in a membership application with a check for your membership fees.

If you have a valid individual membership, the next important step for playing in a USTA league is to secure a team registration number for your entry in a league program. You will need to know a team's number if you are going to register with them on the internet through the USTA Tennis Link program. **Please note that all player registrations for USTA tennis leagues can only be done online.** If you want to organize a team, the USTA website allows players to generate a team registration number through the USTA *Tennis Link* program online at:

http://national.usta.com/leagues/FormsLogin.asp.

In some places, though, you may have to contact the local league coordinator in order to be assigned a team number for use in registration. Once again, the USTA website will help you identify who can help you with this registration process. A local league team registration number is free. However, when players use their team number to register on the team roster, there will be a $3 charge to use the *Tennis Link* program, plus a local league participation fee charged to the player. Have a credit card handy when you register for a team. The only way a player can join a USTA team is to pay online. Since some players do not have a charge card or an online computer, they will have to get someone else to do it for them (usually the team captain).

Unaffiliated individual players who want to join a team can ask the local league coordinator for a referral to an existing team. Another way to find a team is to review the USTA website that lists the names of every team and their complete team rosters. You can identify who the team captains are, then look up their names in a phone directory and call them about joining their teams. When I moved to San Antonio for a six-month work assignment in 2001, I called the local tennis association about joining a league team and they quickly referred me to some team captains who needed players. I got two invitations within 36 hours to play on a team. That is just how easy it can be to get started if you don't know anybody in town.

Please note that some leagues require that all players be enrolled on a team roster before the date of the first league matches. Leagues actually have the local option of allowing players to join teams after the league season begins. Of course you have to be registered on a team before you can play in a league match. The main requirement for all USTA leagues is that team players must have participated in a minimum number of local league matches to be eligible for the annual sectional or national championship tournaments if your team is the league champion.

USTA ADULT LEAGUE PROGRAMS:

The best feature of USTA leagues are the well-developed categories of competition divided according to player ability rating levels and according to age groups. The adult leagues require that players be at least age 19 during the calendar year of team play. There is a senior division for players' ages 50 or older; a super senior division for players 60 and older; and a super senior plus division for players 70 and older. Within these age divisions, there are groupings according to ability levels based on a 1 to 7 rating scale using the National Tennis Rating Program (NTRP). For practical purposes, the rating levels that matter for league play start with the 2.5 rating level and extend up to the 5.0 rating level in most areas, with an open player division offered, too. Typically, the 3.0 rating level is the entry level for good competitive players; the 3.5 rating level is the journeyman level for strong players; the 4.0 and 4.5 rating levels are good enough for some college tennis teams. All the comparisons are relative. The USTA tries to award ratings according to a person's demonstrated playing record. Once match scores are accrued in the Tennis

Link system and a player has a match history recorded over an extended period of time, the ratings become more accurate. When there are disputes about assigned player ratings, a USTA sectional staff member will handle player appeals and team protests.

The team contests in the men and women's **Adult** leagues for ages 19 and older play two courts of singles and three courts of doubles against each other in a match. The team that wins at least three of the five court competitions is the match winner in the league standings. The standings are based on team's match wins and losses for the season. In leagues with a large number of teams, sometimes you play the other teams only once on the schedule. Leagues with six or fewer teams will typically play each other twice or more in a season schedule. **Note: there is no USTA requirement to rank order your players in the match lineup.** You do not have to put your best players in the first court singles match or in the first court doubles matches. Learning how to make competitive lineups for playing under these conditions is a key ingredient for winning in tennis leagues. Lineup strategies are interesting and exciting team considerations, and are the subject of extended discussion in Chapter 3.

The playing formats for men & women's **Senior** (age 50 and up), **Super Senior** (age 60 and up), and **Super Senior Plus** (age 70 and up) leagues consist of matches with three courts of doubles competition. Singles court competition is not required of senior age players in USTA league play. A team victory in these categories requires that one team win at least two of the three courts played. The **Adult Mixed Doubles** league, and **Senior Mixed** doubles league match formats are composed of three courts of competition, too. Thus, it becomes evident that in every category of USTA league play there will be three courts of doubles competition. The importance of doubles play and the development of winning doubles teams is a major topic of discussion in chapter two.

There is one other category of competition for adults available in the USTA **Combo Doubles** leagues. The teams are composed of doubles players with combined levels of rating abilities in divisions of play for 5.5 teams, 6.5 teams, 7.5 teams, and 8.5 teams. For example in the 6.5 combined doubles league, one player could have a 3.0 rating and have a partner who has a 3.5 rating. The rule is that the partners cannot have more than a 1.0 total difference in their ratings. *Please note that this rule about the allowable difference between doubles partners in a combo rating applies to the senior mixed doubles and super senior leagues matches, too.* If you do the math, it becomes apparent that the combinations of ratings will almost always utilize players who have only 0.5 differences in their rating levels. The combo doubles league contests employ three courts of double matches. In the author's home state, the 2006 sectional championships were primarily entered by women's teams. Men have not seemed as interested in this format. One disadvantage of playing in a combo doubles match is that most teams know the secret to victory is to attack the lower rated player on the opposing team. So far, the combo leagues have not gained the same popularity as the other categories of adult competition. There are sectional championships for leagues winners, but there are no national championships for combo teams yet.

The newest USTA playing format is **Tri-Level** league matches. Each team plays one court of 3.5 doubles, one court of 4.0 doubles, and one court of 4.5 doubles. A team must win two out of the three court matches to win the contest. Until this league has more of a playing record for this program, there is no way to tell how popular this format will be over time. For this league to succeed, the USTA will have to offer tri-level competition that includes the 3.0 level players in the lineups. The major limitation for organizing such teams is the availability of players from all three rating levels to form one team.

USTA JUNIOR TEAM TENNIS LEAGUES:

The USTA also has team tennis leagues for junior players. The leagues are divided according to age groups and levels of playing abilities. There are two age categories of competition for boys and girls: **14 & under** and **18 & under**. The three playing levels of competition are **Beginners, Intermediate** (NTRP 3.0 and below), and **Advanced** (NTRP 3.5 and above). Intermediate and advanced league champions can advance to a sectional tournament and a national championship. The USTA website for junior tennis leagues is:

http://teamtennis.usta.com/Main/HomePage.aspx

In some USTA sections, the junior tennis leagues have three schedules of competition within one year: the fall, spring, and summer seasons. Please note that boys and girls play together on the same team. Tennis is spectacularly unique in allowing both genders to combine together on one team, and in having both genders compete against each other in mixed doubles matches. At the sectional tournament, the team matches consist of one boy's singles court, one boys' doubles court, one girl's singles court, one girls' doubles court, and one court of mixed doubles. This format is used for both intermediate and advanced sectional championships. This same format is customarily used for advanced level teams in the local leagues too, but not necessarily for local league intermediate or beginners' teams. The league and sectional team standings are often based on the total games won in all the matches. Check with your junior team tennis league coordinator for the specific rules of competition where you live.

Sometimes the local league competition for beginners and intermediate players uses an expanded playing format that allows more players into the lineup by playing extra courts of singles and doubles play. In one East Texas league, the intermediate and beginners team contests played six courts of singles and three courts of doubles matches using no-add scoring in a pro-set that used a tie-breaker if the score became 7-7 in the game court. Local leagues can allow boys to play against girls in the expanded courts format. The junior tennis team leagues are still developing nationwide and will evolve in time. These leagues are especially valuable for developing players 14 and under since school systems in many places to do not offer organized team competition for middle school and younger players. The USTA junior team leagues can be a great feeder program for local high school varsity programs, and have been used as a junior development program for that purpose in my community tennis association.

United States Professional Tennis Association (USPTA):

http://www.uspta.com/

The United States Professional Tennis Association is the guild of tennis teaching professionals who have organized an interesting league playing format for the recreational playing public. USPTA league programs use smaller team rosters than USTA leagues, a good example of when less is more. A small team roster is always easier to manage, requiring less communication and coordination for matches. A typical match plays only two courts of doubles for a given player rating level. **Note: the USPTA uses the player** ability ratings standards defined by the USTA, and ratings earned in USTA events determine the eligibility for playing in USPTA leagues. A team roster can be as small as six players, making it easier to start up a new team when you don't know a lot of active tennis people. Since it only takes four very good players to be a champion, the USPTA league provides the best opportunity for winning championships for teams that have strength, but not depth, in their stable of players.

The author has often advised tennis groups to develop their program by initially entering teams in a USPTA league. These small roster teams can become the corps for growing the game. The USPTA teams often attract enough other players to tennis that the teams can expand and also play in the USTA leagues that require larger lineups. Once the corps of players is large enough to play in USTA leagues, the problem becomes how to sub-divide into smaller rosters when entering back into a USPTA league. An adult league team in the USTA that uses eight players in a match will usually have enough players to form two USPTA teams. This can be good for growing the sport in general, but it can cause social conflicts when you have to start choosing up sides against each other. These expansion problems are more than offset by the advantages of having access to a larger talent pool from which to form winning tennis teams.

Another attractive feature of USPTA leagues is their cheaper entry fees. The players do not need to be members of the USTA, saving each team member as much as $25 to $40 per year in expenses. In the USPTA, you only have to pay a league participation fee, ranging from $12 to $20 per player. Sometimes a championship team in the USPTA league has to pay another team fee to enter the state championship tournament if the team advances that far in the playoffs. Most winning teams are willing to pay the extra fee for the state tournament when they have become local league champions

The USPTA league playing format is dramatically different than the format used by the USTA. Originally, the USPTA intended that a team would be composed of players for two courts of 3.0 doubles competition, plus two courts of 3.5 doubles, plus another two courts of 4.0 doubles play, and two more courts of 4.5 doubles matches. Each league contest would consist, therefore, of eight courts of multi-level rated matches between two teams. In practice, it has been hard for one group to organize a single team that included players from all the rating levels needed for a match. Consequently, in my area, leagues have been organized that allow teams to enter in divisions based on just one playing rating level. For instance, all of the 3.5 ladies' teams play for a local league championship independent of the other levels of league competition. It has not been necessary that a tennis group have teams entered in all four ratings levels of league play. In this system, each rating level produces a team winner in their league. All four of the rating level champions form an all-star composite team to advance in the USPTA playoff system. Our players enjoy forming alliances with players from other tennis clubs and other communities to represent our region at the state tournament.

The USPTA league's original scoring system was designed to combine the results of every match in the total four-level lineup. The total games won in each set of every court are supposed to be added together for a grand team match total, rather than deciding a match by which team wins the most courts in a match (a problem in itself with an eight courts lineup that could produce a tie.) In my state's championship tournament, a version of this aggregate system is being used. Each court plays a 16 game match and records how many games they have won for their team. Match scores can range from 16-0 to 8-8 to 0-16 for a doubles team. A team could potentially win 128 games in the eight courts of one contest. Once again, two teams could possibly split their games evenly and tie at 64 each. This result is allowable because in the state playoffs the teams keep adding the scores of every match to their cumulative winning totals for the tournament to determine the grand champion. Typically a team will have a four or five match schedule and could amass as many as 540 games in the standings. In this system, every game played is important. Keeping up with the results requires some higher mathematics, but makes for an exciting and intriguing tournament.

While the complicated total games won is feasible in a statewide championship using the full composite team rosters, the sub-divided local league schedules that conduct separate competitions for each player rating level requires a simpler scoring system. In our area, the league standings are based on the number of courts won during the season schedule. As an incentive to put your best players in the first court doubles match, the local league awards five points for winning on court one. The second court doubles match earns three points for the team standings. A team can win as many as eight points against another team, or just five points, or three points, or zero points. Every point earned during the full season is added together to determine the local league team champion who will become part of the all-star composite team that advances to the state championships. **Please note that the USPTA does not conduct a national championship tournament.** This allows each state some latitude in the methods of determining their winners. Always check with your local USPTA league coordinator for information about your local league and state tournament playing schedules and rules of play.

World Team Tennis Leagues (WTT)

www.wtt.com

The World Team Tennis league was founded by Billie Jean King for professional players and public entertainment. Because of the popularity of her innovative playing formats for competition, the WTT has organized competition for recreational players, too. The WTT has a playoff system for local league winners to advance to multi-state regional qualifying tournaments to play in the national championships. The WTT has far fewer local leagues than either the USTA or USPTA programs, which makes it difficult to find available league programs in some areas of the USA. As long as three teams are willing to play together, then you can organize a local league providing you pay the appropriate franchise fees to the WTT. The playing format is distinctive because it requires that a team use both men and women in the lineup. Once again the player ratings standards of the USTA system are used for determining player eligibility for team rosters. Teams with similar player rating levels are grouped together for league competition.

The appealing parts of WTT play are the use of a composite team lineup, the substitution rules allowed during the playing of a set, the scoring system that combines together all the games won in every player's match to determine the team winner, and the come-from-behind opportunity for a team during the final set of the contest. A league match has at least fives sets of competition, and in some formats six sets may be played. The lineup includes one set of men's singles, one set of women's singles, one set of men's doubles, one set of women's doubles, and finishes with at least one set of mixed double (some leagues finish with two sets of mixed doubles, with a designation of which mixed doubles court is the first court team in the lineup.)

The first court (or only court) of mixed doubles competition can be used by the team that is behind in the total games won in the contest to catch up with the overall leading team, providing they win the mixed doubles set score. In this case, the mixed doubles set goes into a sudden death overtime time play. The contending team that won the mixed doubles set must win consecutive games in the overtime without losing any further games to the leading team to keep adding games to their team's composite score. The overtime continues until the contending team catches up evenly with the leading team without losing a game, at which time both teams begin playing a super-tiebreaker. If the leading team wins just one game over the contending team before the composite scores become even, then the overtime ends with the leading team declared the overall winner for the league contest. Of course, if the overall leading team should win in the final set of mixed doubles, the contest has been decided without further match play.

The roster of a WTT entry can use as few as two men and two men in a team match. You can expand the roster and use as many as four men and four women in a five set match. If you play a six set match with two courts of mixed doubles, then you could use five men and five women in the lineup if you so desire. **Note that the most important players on the team are the mixed doubles court partners because they must close out the match.** Be sure to recruit players for your team who are good at mixed doubles.

Remember that you may substitute players during the play of any set. If your player should fall behind by 4-0, you might consider changing the lineup; but the substitute must be able to commence play immediately without benefit of any warm-up. The score keeping compiles a cumulative total of the games won by both teams in the contest. By combining the contributions of each player in the match, the team members actively support each other during the competition. This camaraderie is one of the most enjoyable aspects of WTT league play. Thank you, Ms. King.

Chapter 2   MAKING IT HAPPEN

After winning one of our matches in our tennis league, the players began teasing their team captain about how their victory was "all due to the coaching." Everyone knew full well that the team captain had been busy playing a match during the contest – not coaching. In general, a team captain does everything except coach team players, although a good team captain will arrange for the team to have group lessons with a local tennis pro as needed. What else does a winning team's team captain do? How about all of the following:

TEAM ENTRIES:

When forming a team, the captain needs to contact the league coordinator to find out about the local rules for competition (hopefully they have been published in print copies), and to get on the contact list for information about league meetings and match schedules. The team captain will need to get a team registration number and make sure that the league participation fees for each player on the team roster get paid. Each player enlisted for the team will need to be told how much it will cost to play during the league season, including the prorated team cost of providing balls for the home court matches. Since the USTA has computerized its entire league proceedings, team captains should know how to operate the USTA *Tennis Link* website to register players and enter match scores for those league matches. If the captain is a high-tech challenged person; then, for USTA league team entries, someone must be enlisted who can transact the team's necessary online business. The administrative set-up work for a team to enter a league is absolutely critical, because missing entry deadlines can scrap a whole season before it begins.

RESPECTFULL TEAM MANAGEMENT:

Above all else, the team captain is a personnel manager. Good manners, good organization, and frequent supportive contacts are essential for team building from pre-season recruitment through post-match congratulations or consolations. Inviting players to join a team must be handled as sensitively as courtship and dating, and as diplomatically as selecting members to join an exclusive sorority or fraternity. A team needs only a limited number of players on the roster; and if you are not very careful, there can be hurt feelings about who is included and who is not. **Remember: the way people are treated regarding their tennis interests may affect your social relationships with them all the rest of the year, not just for the season you play together.** Fair play means more than faithfully following the rules of the game; it means treating teammates and opponents courteously and humanely on and off the court even when it might affect your team's winning record.

The most important thing about managing a team is balancing the goal of winning titles with full participation by every player throughout the season's schedule. Even though not everyone one on the team will be of equal ability, everyone must be treated as being equally important to the success of the team. Use as a firm abiding principle that **if someone is good enough to be on the team, then they are good enough to play in the lineup on a regular basis like everyone else.** Do not recruit players just to be occasional substitutes, even if the player offers to join the team on that basis. Always assume that people join a tennis team because they want to play matches. Team morale depends upon frequent participation in the lineup. If you accept someone as a team member, there is an inherent obligation to include them in the lineups. Players need to be used in at least two out of every three matches on the schedule, and should not be involuntarily left out of the lineup for two consecutive matches.

Team members need to keep in mind that player development comes from court experience. There is only way for anyone to become good enough to be a winner, and that is to play matches. Some people believe that you already have to have good skills to be in a team's lineup. Actually, the truth of tennis is that you have to play in lineups to have the chance of becoming good. Only match play gives us the kind of experience that counts. Even though we may lose to better players at first, the more often we play "up," the sooner we will move "up" in our game and will eventually "catch" up enough with the champs to beat them. Good teams evolve over time and adopt the perspective that Rome wasn't built in one day. Be patient with each other and good things will eventually come to those who build for the future, if not this season then in the next ones.

Another guiding principle for personnel management is that **once someone is a member of a team, that player will expect to be a member of the team in future league entries. Add members to your team as if they will be perpetual members of the roster** (as long as the players have been compatible with their teammates and dependable about team schedules). Team captains shouldn't operate as if each new league season means that all the playing positions on the roster are completely open, thereby requiring tryouts to make the team again. Overly competitive persons may believe that a "no cut" policy will hamper their chances of winning; but this is not necessarily true. A team can respect tenure and also win through thoughtful initial personnel selection and good utilization of available team talent. Conversely, individual players should always be treated as "free agents" who have the right to play with any team they might want to join. They might want to play with you again, or they might want to play with someone else next time. Just be grateful for the season they are your teammate, and always wish them well in their future matches. Personal respect for each player engenders strong team loyalty and helps to build a strong core of committed players. Teams need human "glue" to stay together; winning dynasties are formed this way.

IF YOU BUILD IT, THEY WILL COME:

Sometimes a start-up team needs to attract enough players to have a full roster. In which case, the attitude can be "come one, come all." In these start-from-scratch situations, personnel selection can be very inclusive. As soon as someone is willing to assume the responsibility for organizing a team, simply announce the team's formation and publicize who is the contact person. When someone joins the team, they can be used to help recruit other players. The good-old-boy and good-old-girl network can be really effective in filling up a team quickly. Some club pros report that there are usually far more players interested in joining teams than there are teams available to take them. If you want to have a team, the players will find you once they know how.

Even an established team will need replacement players occasionally. The team captain must politely indicate whether there are any openings to interested prospects who may contact them about joining an existing team. Please do not be guilty of dropping someone from a roster in order

22

to make room for someone who may be a better player and make a stronger teammate. You might be tempted to add the new hot prospect by expanding the size of the team roster, but a larger membership means decreasing the frequency of playing times for the veteran players – an unwise move unless everyone on the team has agreed to the extra acquisition and its consequences.

Most players know that championships are won in the off-season. The decisions made about who will be on your team will affect your season record more than any coaching or lineup change that can be made once the league matches begin. Everyone wants to have good players on their team, which makes recruitment become all-important to your team's eventual success. In so far as is possible, a prospective player should play some practice matches with somebody on the team before they are invited to join the team. Don't let the prospect know that the practice match is a team tryout session since you might not want to add them to your team. If you do meet someone with real talent, tell them about your team and introduce them to your team members so they can decide if they would like to play with you. Remember, if they are a good player, they will want to know about the abilities of their prospective teammates as much as you are seeking to add winners to your team roster.

If you are forming a title contending team, then you will be well advised to enlist players who will be available when your team advances to the playoffs. Tell your recruits in advance when and where the championships will be played, and ask if they can go with the team to these events if your team is the local champion. You will not be presumptuous to advise your team about the prospective dates for sectional, state, and national championship tournaments. Sometimes players' work schedules or family responsibilities will limit their availability when you will need them the most. You will have to factor that into your team composition to be sure that you will have enough good players on your traveling roster

ROSTER SIZES AND COMPOSTION:

The formula for a team size depends upon how many people are used in a match lineup. The maximum workable team size is one and half times the number of players to be used in a team contest. In USTA adult leagues (ages 19 and older), a total of eight players are needed to enter the two singles matches and three doubles matches. Such an adult team roster can include as many as twelve players and a minimum of ten players. The ideal roster would have three singles players and eight doubles players, making a total of eleven people on the team. If all the players participate equally, every one may play in the lineup at least two out of three team contests. Using the same formula for the size of other type league entries, rosters for USTA mixed doubles teams, senior and super senior teams that require six players to play three courts of doubles should have rosters of eight players (nine players is the limit). Teams in USPTA leagues that use lineups with only two courts of doubles should have six players on their roster. WTT entries can use as many as four men and four women on their team roster.

Extra members are needed on teams because tennis players are unavailable from time to time. There is nothing worse than having to default a match in a lineup because you can't get enough people to play at a given time on your schedule. Teams need extra players on the roster for several reasons. Not every new recruit to league tennis will like the necessary routines to be available for team matches. Even the best of teams will have player dropouts once in a while.

Regrettably, reliable veteran players will also be absent due to illness, work schedules, or competing family special occasions. Playing injuries occur often enough that your team will unfortunately lose the services (and volleys, too) of valuable team members. In the senior and super senior age team leagues for instance, it gets more and more difficult to keep a healthy lineup intact for the entire season. You might observe at senior team practices that there are more elbow and knee braces on the court than people.

Sometimes a team gets more prospective players than the team can use. In these situations you have the opportunity to help grow the sport -- a major goal of tennis these days. It is actually in our self-interest to give something back to the game by making referrals to other teams, or helping organize new teams to accommodate all of the interested players who want to play in leagues. There are many average level players who would be grateful just to play on a regular basis in some organized program. Helping them form a team or find a team might actually give your team an opposing team when you can use your own team substitutes in a winning situation. In the author's own community, a few leading team members consult with each other before the start of a new league season to estimate how many people are known to be interested in playing on somebody's team. By collaborating together each year, enough teams can be organized to insure that no one is left out of the game. We stress that being a regular starter on some team is usually more desirable than being underutilized as a substitute with a championship team. The prevailing attitude is that everyone in our town wants to be champions, but winning is not the sole reason we play the game.

OUTFITTING THE TEAM:

Team uniforms are entirely optional, but a very nice way to form a team identity. Matching jerseys are popular in women's leagues, and add a sense of style to court dress. Players enjoy designing their court clothing and like adding team logos, nicknames and mascots decorations to their outfits. Although men may be less fashion conscious, they can be induced to get into the spirit of the game with their own distinctive dress. Spectators really appreciate being able to identify who belongs to the same team when the players are on the courts in their league matches.

ABOUT PLAYER RATINGS:

Recruiting team members requires thorough familiarity with the player rating standards developed by the USTA. Their system uses a seven point rating system for defining the levels of playing ability known as the National Tennis Rating Program (NTRP). Ratings are the basis for grouping players of similar abilities in league programs. The system tries to index players on an objective basis, but all the comparisons are relative ones. The NTRP is not arbitrary, but certainly has a subjective element in it - somewhat like grading on the curve. The dividing line between a 3.0 player and 3.5 players is often hard to discern. The more you study the patterns of player rating changes, the more confounded you may become in trying to determine what rating level a person should have on a team.

For one thing, the USTA keeps confidential the formula used to compute a player's rating. Supposedly a player's rating level is averaged after every match score is entered in the tennis link database. All players have a rolling record that is used to estimate whether they are properly rated and still eligible to play in a given division of league play. The system is designed to disqualify someone if the record indicates that the player is overrated for the league they have entered. If a player wins three "benchmark" matches in one season (wins over USTA recognized good players), then they can be promoted to a higher level immediately and disqualified out of the league they had entered. The USTA grants benchmark status in its annual player ratings to all those who have played in the current year's sectional championships for adult division teams. There are no warnings given to a team or to an individual player that someone's rating is growing too high for the league they have entered. Furthermore, no player is ever told their exact playing average. You will only know what your particular category of playing ability is. After a while, players begin to introduce themselves to each other by their current rating level.

The classification of new players within the NTRP has been the biggest single problem in using the rating scheme for league play. The USTA initially uses a self-rating method that relies upon a player's self-report about their playing experience to estimate what should be their rating level. Players do not always know how to index themselves properly, and sometimes will under or over report their aptitudes because they do not have recent court experience for an accurate self-rating. Some years ago, the USTA required that new players be evaluated by a professional tennis teacher. Even though this rating method would seem to have been more accurate, some pros have reported that players would hide their true abilities during their evaluation (like playing with their non-dominate hand) or ask for special consideration in the rating they would be given. In general, when enlisting a new person for league play, have them be conservative about how they estimate their playing level until they have a chance to compare themselves in practice matches with other players of well known rating abilities. League competition has escalated through the years so that today's standards are almost one full level higher than they were a decade ago. Today some 3.0 players could have won in yesteryear's 3.5 league play.

Players are allowed to make appeals of the ratings they have been assigned. The USTA *Tennis Link* has an automated online ratings appeal process that will give an immediate decision about a rating's appeal. After the mid-year and the end-of-year ratings are published, you may also submit a written appeal to your sectional headquarters asking for a revision of your rating to a lower level. Until the automated appeal system is implemented, all appeals will have to be in writing. If your rating level is only .05 higher than the upper limit for your playing division, then you can be reclassified back to the lower level. If a player is age 60 or older, you are given a larger allowance of .10 points above a rating level in the appeals process. If your players should get a ratings promotion, encourage them to file an appeal since they have about a 50% chance of getting it approved. There is an advantage of keeping the lower rating. The eligibility rules always allow any player the privilege of entering a league program that is above their personal rating level. You increase your playing options by getting an appeal approved. If maintaining a rating status is important for peer acceptance, then use the ratings promotion as a recognized indicator of your improved playing abilities

SINGLES PLAYERS ARE CRUCIAL IN ADULT LEAGUES:

The USTA Adult leagues formats require that teams play two courts of singles and three courts of doubles in a match. Players in the adult leagues need only be age 19 or older (to be eligible, your 19th birthday may occur anytime during the calendar year of the league schedule). If you are going to be truly competitive within this age group, veteran players are fond of saying that "you had better recruit some flat bellies" for the singles matches if you want to win. How true, how true! The most frequently debated issue among adult teammates concerns who can play and win the singles matches. Both skill and conditioning are needed for the singles matches. Older veteran players (if healthy) can be very competitive in doubles matches against any age opponent during most of their careers. Singles matches are a different proposition because strength and speed are important for covering the whole court by yourself. Some people prefer to play singles because they can keep up with the rhythm of the game easier. A singles player can get by with a good serve and good ground strokes, and not have to have an all court game that uses volleys, too. Some people's personalities are more solitary and are better in a singles match. Concentrate on recruiting singles players for your team foremost because two good players can give you two court victories in singles matches, whereas two good players can only give you only one court victory in doubles. Besides that, doubles players are easier to find to fill out a roster because 80% of adult recreational tennis is played in doubles matches. Ideally, you would like to have three very capable singles players on your adult team roster to use in your lineups; but rarely does a team have this much talent to spare for the singles courts.

IN DOUBLES 1 + 1 DOES NOT ALWAYS EQUAL 2:

Putting two good players together on the same court in a doubles match does not necessarily produce a winning team. Likewise, sometimes two players can become partners and play better than either one of them does individually. Everybody wants a good player for his or her partner. Pairing good players together is only part of the process. Partners must not only be good players, but they must be the right player for a given person's playing abilities and playing style. Forming doubles partnerships is like mating skunks. If you are not careful, you can create a big stink instead of a lasting love affair. Invite the whole team to play a series of short doubles matches where they change partners after a mini-match together. Rotate the partnerships until everyone has played at least once with every other team member. The captain should keep count of how many games each person won during the round robin rotation with other partners. You will get a good estimate of the relative strengths of the doubles players in such a practice session. You might also discover that some combinations work better together than other partner pairings do. This practice procedure creates team bonding and provides the roster with introductions to each other's playing abilities.

After the team members have practiced with each other, the captain needs to interview privately the players who will be used in the doubles lineup about their preferences for a doubles partner. Most players will politely say that they are willing to play with anyone, so phrase the question in terms of which partner would give the player the best chance of winning in doubles matches. Ideally, players would have established their own partnerships before joining the team. In the absence of existing partnerships, the players should be paired with someone of equivalent ability. Try to keep the same players together as partners during the league season so they can develop and improve their court relationship. Nevertheless, have a team understanding that every doubles player needs to have an alternate partner in case of absences or tactical necessity.

When forming doubles partnerships find out which players can defend the "add" side (left) of the court when receiving service, and make sure that every doubles team has one such player in their lineup to play this role. Keep in mind that doubles teams are somewhat like volleyball teams in that you also need "setup" people and "spikers" for effective combinations. At least one doubles partner should have an aggressive net game for a team to succeed, and they will need a partner who knows how to build a winning point. One other consideration for partnerships is the temperament of the people in the lineup. Some tennis players are very internal and need a quiet partner so they can stay inner focused during play. Other players respond to court chatter and encouragement during the contest. Sports psychology is a marvelous thing and good teams resolve these issues one way or another.

Tactically, try to build an anchor doubles team by pairing your strongest players together to form a team that can dominate your opposition on the lead doubles court. Ideally, you would like to have at least one court that can win against anybody. The certainty of their victory will inspire the rest of your team and instill confidence in them, too. A powerful doubles team gives the rest of your roster some excellent competition in your team practices, thereby building them up in the process. Conversely, do not dilute your team strength by trying to stretch your talent by mistakenly pairing your strongest players with less able players in hopes that the strong players can carry the other players to victory. In doubles, this is an invitation to defeat. Your opponents will quickly attack the weaker partner in your doubles matches. The strong players can't cover the whole court by themselves. Realistically, the strong player will only serve once every four games. Your doubles team will only be assured of winning about two games a set, and could lose 6-2, 6-2 to an opponent who knows how to divide and conquer.

MIXED DOUBLES DEPENDS UPON THE LADIES:

Forming mixed doubles partnerships is like dating – the women on a team must be satisfied about which men may become their partners. The ladies' preferences about partnerships are paramount for team harmony and success. Court relationships are usually more important to the women on a team than they are to the men on the roster. The gentlemen are usually deferential to the ladies on a team, and may be expected to agree to play with whoever becomes their partner. More importantly, the team that has the best women's players will win the most matches. Experience has shown that if one team has the best men and another team has the best women, the team with the best women will be the likely winners. Concentrate on enlisting good women for your team and the men's part of the lineup will take care of itself.

A CAPTAIN'S PLACE IN THE LINEUP:

Magnanimous team captains will frequently sacrifice their own playing opportunities for the sake of increasing participation by the other team members. To have an effective team roster, maybe the team captain shouldn't be the best player on the squad since they might elect to sit out more of the matches than their quota (modesty about one's abilities and utilization is endearing to other players and promotes team morale). Quite frankly, being a team captain almost ensures that you will not be playing at your best on the team because of the pre-match distractions about team management. Getting players to the courts on time, scouting out the other team, decision making about the lineups, greeting the opposing team and giving out court assignments, keeping up with scores and reporting the results, requires a lot of time and attention. If a team can afford the luxury of a non-playing captain, it removes some stress from one of the contestants -- thereby improving their court play and chances of winning.

Team captains will be well advised to sacrifice themselves in the lineup on those occasions when the lineup strategy is to gain advantage over another team by shifting their playing personnel in their court assignments to where they can win a majority of the courts, but not all of them. In those situations, somebody on your team may have to be deliberately paired against a strong opponent who will be favored to win over them. If the captain is playing in that match's lineup, then the captain should play on the court that is likely to get beat. However, a captain should never admit to a partner if he or she expects to be defeated. Who knows, you might upset the better team. Never automatically concede a victory to anyone before play begins. Always make the other team earn their points the old fashioned way by having to outplay you, not by giving in to them because you think they are better than you.

PRACTICES:

The most important practices occur before the season begins. In the open adult leagues, the captain needs to know who can play effective singles matches and who will be compatible doubles partners. Everyone should be invited to try out for the singles positions on the roster since an open adult team is built upon winning the singles court contests. Interested singles players should be asked to compete in a round robin series of challenge matches with each other to determine their team rankings. Even if the captain has a good estimate of the players' relative abilities, the challenge match records are the fairest way to establish playing priorities and avoid the appearance of favoritism. Challenge matches help the players recognize and accept their earned places in the lineup. Always practice super-tiebreakers in every session of singles and doubles matches.

After the season begins, it is not necessary that all the team members practice together at the same time. Simultaneous group practice might make the captain feel more secure about the team's preparedness, but it is not necessary for the individual players unless they need help in getting someone to practice with them at a given time in a given place. The team captain should offer a regular meeting time for those who want to be there, and then presume that the other players will make their own practice arrangements as they desire. Practice is not the same as taking tennis lessons from someone. If a coach wants to promote player development, the emphasis should be upon encouraging players to get individual help with their skills and strokes from someone who can improve the way they play the game.

TEAM SUPPLIES:

Even though all players are supposed to provide their own uniforms and equipment, someone has to remember to:
1. Supply the match balls when you are the home team.
2. Measure the net heights to be sure they are not too high or too low according to USTA standards.
3. Racquet strings break often enough during matches that the players need to have extra racquets available on the court for immediate use to be able to continue play without delay.
4. Have some a small supply of first aide items at courtside, to include band-aids and pain relievers. For quick non-medical relief of heat exhaustion or muscle cramps, a well known home remedy is drinking dill

pickle juice. One sun-belt area team takes chilled bottles of the yellow fluid to their matches and joking tell other teams that they drink "Eau de Seabisket" to stay strong. Shades of Mahatma Gandhi.

PLAYER UTILIZATION:

If you want to keep players motivated and available, use them frequently. By all means, publish the proposed team lineups to your players well in advance of each contest. Your teammates want to know if they are going to get to play; and need a chance to respond to you about their playing availability or satisfaction with their utilization (especially about who will be partners in the doubles matches, or whether they feel adequate to play in a singles match). If you use the suggested quotas for team size memberships, then you can let your very best players stay in the lineup for almost every match on the first singles court and/or the first doubles court. The remaining players will get to play at least every other match, and possibly two out of three matches.

There is a practical way to compute mathematically how often your players can be used in a league schedule. Count how many players are on your team; then count how many players may be used in the lineup for one match. Count how many matches your team will play on its schedule and multiple that number times the number of players who are used in a lineup. For instance, in an USTA adult league, a team uses eight (8) players in each match. If your team plays a schedule of six (6) matches, then you would use a total of 48 players for the season. If your team had twelve (12) players on the roster, then everyone could play in exactly four (4) matches.

Looking ahead to the time when your team advances to a state/sectional/national championship tournament, keep in mind that teams are usually grouped into four-team flights and play a three-match, round robin schedule. Once again you need to do some math and compute how often your players may participate in these championships. The size of your team roster is the determining factor in planning for player utilization. Players should be used in at least two out of the three matches to make their travel time and expenses worth making the trip with the team during the playoffs. Furthermore, there is a frequency of participation in some championship tournaments that affects a player's eligibility to play in the next higher level of the playoffs. As an example, in the USTA super senior division of competition, each player must have been used in at least two matches during the season, one of which has to be at the sectional level to advance to the nationals. In some rating categories, teams are allowed to go directly from a local district to the sectional tournament if they did not have any local opponents. In those special circumstances, the team roster must be small enough to use everyone at least twice in the sectional event. The ideal roster size for a senior or super senior team is eight (8) players when everybody plays in at least two out of three matches, and two players may be used in all three matches.

The next task is to find out if and when your players might not be available for a given play date. You will have to keep track of all this information on a calendar to know when a given player might have to rotate into or out of the lineups. You will even have to track player availability during a championship tournament because, believe it or not, there will be times when someone can't be in the lineup even then. Finally, you have to estimate how strong the opposing teams are on your schedule and calculate when you need to have your very best players in the lineup, and when you can afford to let everyone else play their matches. The study of tactical composition of lineups for matches is a subject all of its own, and will be covered in depth in Chapter 3.

LINEUP STRATEGIES

Winning USTA league matches often depends upon your choice of players for a lineup and their respective deployment on the courts. USTA rules count a win on every court as being of equal value, and allow teams the latitude of putting their best players anywhere in the lineup. Team captains must write down their lineups before a match without knowing what lineup the opposing team will be using. The captains exchange lineups with each other and begin the match. Players on both teams are vitally interested in knowing who will be playing against each other. Each team tries to anticipate what their chances of winning on each court will be, and calculate whether their team can win most of the courts in the matchups. Some teams leave the pairings up to chance and hope for the best. If you have great talent on your team, you might be able to prevail against all odds without regard to where your people play against a given opponent. Otherwise, you would like to design your lineups so your team will have an advantage over the opposition in the majority of the matches and thereby claim the team victory.

To gain an advantage for your lineup in a given match you will need to know two important things: what are the true differences in the playing abilities of your teammates, and who will likely be in your opposing lineup, including what their playing records are. Assessing your own team should be easy enough if your players have had enough practice matches against each other to establish a true pecking order among themselves before the start of the season. Even then, you might be surprised at the different conclusions some teams make about how they self-rate each other. Hopefully, your team will have a consensus about who can do what for the team, while publicly respecting each other's reputations. The important thing is to know the strength and depth of your players' abilities for constructing your lineups at any given time. Some teams have a few invincible superstars where the key factor is choosing where to use them in the lineup for the best advantage. Other teams may have a solid corps of good players who can win matches most of the time, if not all of them. Team depth in a lineup is just as important for winning as the strength of your best players. The lineup strategies for a deep team may be different than for a team with a few strong individual players. Occasionally, a team will be both strong and deep in its abilities, in which case you may start making advance reservations for the national championships.

Not only do you have to plan for each contest from week to week, but you also have to estimate the relative strength of all the teams in your league or playoff flight of championship competition. As the season progresses it will be easier to assess who the league contenders are and who the pretenders are. Of necessity, you have to plan for the rotation of players in and out of your lineup. Most captains will have in mind an "A" team lineup, and alternate lineups that use some substitutes. The substitutes will be used against your weaker opponents or in lineups where you can afford to take risks on one of the courts in the lineup. The use of substitutes requires diplomacy because you never want to degrade your own players for fear of hurting their morale and playing self-confidence. More importantly, you don't want to make it obvious to your opponents that there are obvious distinctions about your team's playing abilities.

The main considerations for choosing your team lineup are your opponent's abilities, and the playing formations they use in their matches. You can either guess what will happen, or you can take the time to study the playing records of your opponents and make an informed decision about what lineup will work best against them. Such pre-match planning of lineups can be the most exciting and important thing anyone does to help their team win, and it is often the difference maker in becoming a champion. The author has developed a systematic method for scouting opponents which he publishes to his team before each match so they will know what to expect on game day (this system will be explained and illustrated in Chapter 4). Like most forecasts, teams enjoy comparing the lineup projections against the actual lineup they face to see how well they have anticipated the match ups. Such preparedness instills confidence in a team about their prospects for winning. One such team member once boasted to an associate that his team captain knew what the other team had eaten for breakfast because he had read their mail and eavesdropped on their nightmares. If only that were actually true, matches could be won on paper and not have to be played on courts.

For the purposes of lineup analysis and court strategies, use the following terms of reference about player strengths and court assignments. Designate the relative abilities of the players in your lineup by numerical order. Refer to the best entries in your lineup as either singles player #1 or doubles team #1. Refer to your second best entries as either singles player #2 or doubles team #2. In doubles matches refer to your third best entry as team #3. When you write down your lineup for the official score card, the entry form will require that you assign players to specific courts for their matches. On the form you must list who plays on the first and second court singles matches (if you are playing in a USTA adult league), and you must list who will play on the first, second, and third court doubles matches. **Remember: the USTA rules for player court assignments do not require that a team put their players in their descending order of abilities on their corresponding court number.** According to these rules you could randomly draw the names of your players out of a hat and write them down in any order that you please. The only requirement is that you cannot change the order of play once you submit it to the scorekeeper or to the opposing team captain.

LINEUP FORMATIONS

If you assign your players according to their descending order of relative abilities to the playing courts in the order listed on a score form, then the shorthand notation for such a lineup would be 1-2-3 on the three courts. This formation is labeled a "**straight**" lineup. Since the rules allow a team to assign their players to any designated court of the lineup, when a team uses their best #1 player(s) on either the second or third court then the lineup arrangement is labeled a "**stacked**" formation. There are several variations of how a lineup may be stacked. If the best player(s) are assigned to the second court, the lineup options are 2-1-3 or 3-1-2. If the best player(s) are assigned to the third court, then the lineup options are 3-2-1 or 2-3-1. If the best player(s) are left on the first court, there is one stacked lineup variation that can be used that puts the second best player(s) on the third court in a 1-3-2 formation.

There are advantages to each of these playing plans, and circumstances when each formation is the best alignment for your team to use against a given opponent. Stacked lineups are used to gain advantages on a majority of the courts, either to clinch a victory for a strong team or to counter a very strong person at some position in the lineup of the opposing team. Sometimes a team uses an irregular formation because the opposing team uses stacked lineups and you must counter their lineup moves. Using strategy in these situations is a tactical guessing game that taxes the ingenuity of a good team captain. There are several variations of stacked lineups you might use in doubles. In USTA adult league there is only one variation for using the singles court players. Here are some considerations for using straight and stacked lineup formations in your matches.

THE STRAIGHT LINEUP:

The formula is 1-2 in singles and 1-2-3 in doubles for a straight lineup when you deploy the best players on the first court, the second best players on the second court, and the third best players on the third court. Many teams implicitly presume that a straight lineup is the norm for competition; but that is not what the rules state or playing etiquette requires. A straight lineup works anytime your team has a known superiority over another squad. In which case, use the "straight" ahead power play for the victory. For a straight formation to work well tactically, your best players (the "A" team) should be in the lineup. Teams are mostly likely to use a straight formation in the opening match of a league season to test the strength of their roster to find out just how good their team can be. Teams will often use a straight lineup when in doubt about an opponent's abilities or lineup patterns. **Remember: a team that always uses a straight lineup is vulnerable to defeat by an opponent's stacked lineup if the other team can be certain of how your team will be deployed.** On the other hand, every team should occasionally use a straight lineup as part of an overall season strategy of varying the use of their team players to keep other teams from easily anticipating what to expect from your team. Sometimes you will risk using a straight lineup in one match in order to disguise your intentions of using a stacked lineup when you play an important opponent later on in your schedule.

THE SINGLES SWITCH:

Instead of lining up in a straight 1-2 singles courts formation, a team can switch their best player to the second court in a 2-1 alignment. **If an adult team wants to win a contest in USTA play, they must plan on winning at least one of the two singles courts** (the lineup will also have to win two out of the three doubles courts). The singles switch formation gives a team a better chance of claiming at least one singles court victory, a sound reason for stacking this part of the lineup. Your opponent may have a virtually unbeatable star singles player who should be avoided, in which case the switch is a good move. The author's 2005 adult division men's team used this move to win the finals of the sectional championships to upset a team that had the state's #1 ranked singles player who usually played on the first court for his team. Another reason to use the singles switch lineup is to give your second best singles player some good experience and find out how strong their playing abilities may be for future reference. By switching your singles court assignments you can express confidence in your players and confuse your opposing team about the tactics you will use in future matches against them.

THE DOWNWARD SLIDE:

In the doubles court matches, the downward slide formation moves the best players to the second court, the second best players move to the third court, and the third best players go to the first court in the 3-1-2 slide. Your third best players on the first court are deliberately placed at a disadvantage in their match-ups in order to gain advantages on the second and third courts. The players who knowingly accept their first court mis-match will sometimes refer to their assignment as "taking one (a loss) for the team." **The "slide" lineup is the best counter move against a straight formation and is the most popular stacked lineup used in league matches.** The author's senior mixed doubles won a league championship in a four match series against a team that was unbeatable on the first court (the author's team used four different mixed doubles teams on the first court and all of them lost). The opposing team won the first contest when both teams used a straight lineup against each other. In the next three matches, the author's team shifted into a downward slide formation and won by 2-1 in the succeeding three matches because the other team never varied their lineup and stayed in a straight alignment.

THE SEMI-SLIDE:

You can counter an opposing team that is known to use the downward slide formation by putting your best team on the second court and your second best team on the first court in a 2-1-3 alignment. The formation requires that your team's best doubles players be able to win against most good opponents. In those circumstances you are trying to deliberately pair your strongest players against the other team's strength in order to neutralize the opponent's attempt to maneuver their players into a better winning position against your team. **When you have a dominant first court doubles team, you go hunting for the other team's best players to beat them**. Taking command of the middle doubles court with your best players puts pressure on other teams where they will usually deploy some of their better players. In case you have prepared to combat a downward sliding opponent with this counter move and face a different formation than expected, the partial slide lineup will still work if you have a third best doubles team that is usually competitive with the third best players on other teams.

THE MIDDLE SAG:

The middle sag lineup places the best players on the first and third courts, and the third best players take the second court in either a 1-3-2 or 2-3-1 formation. **Most teams protect their middle court (court 2) and will keep some of their playing strength in that position.** If you want a fairly certain plan that will avoid part of an opponent's strength, then use a sag formation. The **"reverse sag"** (2-3-1) is a good counter move against an opponent who you think will use the "downward slide" (3-1-2) against you. There is a calculated risk in using the reverse sag formation that can be offset by using the **"simple sag"** (1-3-2) formation, providing you have a reliable first court doubles team of winning players. The simple sag works well for teams that have some strength at the top of their lineup, and will work against an opponent who uses either a straight lineup or a slide formation against your team. The simple sag might actually appear to look like a straight lineup to an opponent who is not thoroughly familiar with your players' different abilities. In advanced tennis matches at the championship level of competition, the simple sag can be used to deceive a future opponent into expecting a straight lineup from your team when you plan to surprise that opponent with a slide in your lineup. Tennis tactics can become a highly mental game of trying to outguess each other in making lineups.

THE REVERSE FLIP:

Flipping a lineup means having the best players and the

third best players switch courts in a 3-2-1 reverse formation lineup. The "**flip**" works if your second best players can control the middle court match, and is used if you can catch an opponent using a sag formation. The flip can be used against a team that has more depth than strength in their lineup. This formation is used infrequently. In the 2003 senior mixed doubles sectional championships, the author's team had a re-match with a strong and deep team with a predictable lineup. His team knew they could win the second court match-up, and had a higher probability of winning on the third court than the first court if the flip were used. If you have a clear idea of your probable match-ups, the flip may be necessary for a win. You might use this lineup in a relatively safe match just to confuse future opponents who are known to study your team's playing patterns.

LINEUP CONSIDERATIONS:

After a while, making out lineups becomes like a game of scissors, rocks and paper as teams plot the anticipated moves of their opponents. You have to be careful not to outsmart yourself in choosing a lineup. A carefully planned stacked lineup should gain one more court win for your team than you would have earned if you had used a straight lineup instead. Every lineup (straight or stacked) has an element of risk in it regardless of what you choose to do, and that is what makes tennis so exciting and interesting. You can improve your chances of winning a team match by keeping in mind the following dictums:

• In order to win BIG, someone good on your team will have to beat somebody good on the other team. Winning teams are not afraid of competition. At the championship level there aren't any weak opponents. Plan as if you will play against the opposing team's strongest people in your match with them.

- Most teams (including your own) will protect the middle doubles court (#2) with some of their better players. You know where to find part of a team's strength to challenge it or to avoid it.

- Teams that habitually follow the same lineup formation are inviting defeat by opponents who study their playing patterns. You must vary the lineups you use in the course of a season schedule, even in the playoffs.

- Your considered choice of a lineup may only result in a stand-off with the opposing team, with neither team gaining an advantage or a disadvantage in the court pairings.

Chapter 4

SCOUTING REPORTS

Your lineup formation works best if it is based on how your opponents will be using their talent in their lineups. Even on an informal basis, most teams are interested in what to expect in the matches they are about to play. Since 2002, the USTA has made this easier to determine through the individual and team playing records stored in their *Tennis Link* archives. An enterprising student of the game can learn to scout opponents by studying each opposing player's league win/loss records, their playing position in their team's court assignments, and who have been their doubles partners in the lineup. The author specializes in preparing written summaries of all this information for his teammates. These reports have become so helpful that other teams have asked for similar consultations and scouting reports for their forthcoming matches, especially when they advance to the playoffs. You can prepare your own useful reports if you are willing to spend some time researching the USTA database and make notes about what you learn.

ROSTER SIZES AND UTILIZATIONS:

Start your scouting report by printing out the full roster of the team you are going to analyze. Count how many players are registered on the team and evaluate how frequently they can use their full roster in the number of matches they have on their schedule. Take notice of a team that has too many or too few players on the team, using the guidelines suggested for team compositions in Chapter 2. Pay attention to how often each player appears in the lineups and who the team relies upon the most in their matches. In the midst of a league playing season, if you keep count of how often players are being used, sometimes you can project when an opposing team might have to use some of their substitutes in order to keep them eligible for the subsequent league or sectional playoffs. There is also a minimum requirement of playing at least once in a sectionals tournament to participate in the USTA national championships.

Consider the following example: a Cowtown senior women's team won their league despite having an unusually large roster of 15 women on their team. The senior league only uses six players at a time in league matches. The Cowtown team played an eight-match league schedule and had to make frequent rotations of their large roster in and out of the lineup so every one could play at least twice to be eligible for the playoffs. After winning their league, these senior women had a two-match city playoff. During these two city matches, the team used only seven different women in their lineups, thereby leaving out half of their team (eight women) from the city playoffs (which they won). Subsequently, these senior ladies advanced to the sectional playoffs where they used only nine different women in their flight's three-match schedule, once again leaving out six of their roster from these important matches. Whether the team is too large or not, the playing frequency of the roster is pertinent. The more often a player is used, the more likely you will play against them in their lineup. Pay special attention to whether someone is used in crucial matches or in the playoffs to get an estimate of who are the key players on the other team.

CHECK PLAYER RATINGS:

After compiling the participation record of the team you are scouting, look up the NTRP rating for each player if a mid-year rating has been published for your leagues before you play this team. You might also look up each player's rating for the previous year to see if they had recently been promoted into your playing level; or see if they used to have a higher rating than your current league program but were moved down because of a rating appeal or borderline performances. If your team advances to your area's championships, you will likely have the additional mid-year ratings information available to guide you in evaluating your opponents. Later, after you have played the team, go back and check the final adjusted ratings of your opponent at the end of the calendar year. You may face this team again, and the comparisons will help you gain perspective about your own team's abilities for future reference. **Winning teams (yours and theirs) will be composed of strong players who will get promoted to higher rating levels because of their match records.**

Consider the example of the 2004 metroplex men's league senior division team that had already won the adult division sectional USTA championship. Five veterans of the adult league roster also played for the metroplex team during their sectional senior men's tournament (which they ended up winning). By researching the ratings and league experiences of this senior men's roster, the following scouting report was made about their NTRP profiles to identify the team leaders.

METROPLEX CHAMPS SENIOR MEN
RATING RECORD

	Starting Rating	Mid-Year Rating	End-Year Rating	Adult Team Vet
Robert B.	3.0	3.0	3.0	Yes
Tom B.	3.0	3.0	4.0	
Dennis R.	3.0	3.0	3.5	Yes
Joseph H.	3.0	3.0	3.5	
Boris G.	3.0	3.5	3.5	
Pat R.	3.0	3.5	4.0	Yes
Ichiro F.	3.0	3.0	3.5	Yes
Rick B.	3.0	3.0	3.5	
Mike M.	3.0	3.5	3.5	Yes

After compiling the starting ratings and the mid-year ratings, the advance scouting report about the metroplex senior men noted that five players on this nine-man roster had also been members of the metroplex adult men's team that had just won the sectional championship. These five players were bolded to identify those men who had been good enough to win in the younger age division of competition. Two of these senior men (**Pat R. & Mike M.**) had been valuable enough to have played in the metroplex adult men's starting lineup during the team's semi-final and final sectional championship matches and had won both times. **Pat R.** was cited as the "go to" player on the senior men's team. At mid-year the senior team had three players known to have been promoted to the 3.5 rating level. Subsequently, the metroplex adult team and senior team both won the national USTA championships. As a result, seven of these senior men were promoted to higher playing levels in the final end-of-year ratings; two men (**Tom B. and Pat R.**) were extra elevated to the 4.0 level, and five men were elevated to the 3.5 level for the next year.

INDIVIDUAL WIN/LOSS RECORDS:

Next, compute the individual win/loss record for each player on the team you are scouting; and make a separate comparison for singles matches and doubles matches. The *Tennis Link* lists the complete year-long record for each USTA player. Compile each person's record for only the specific league your team has entered. Many players enter multiple categories, including teams in two different rating levels of competition. The sum total of a player's match experience is useful for evaluating that player's overall abilities, but concentrate just on the season record in the league of particular interest. You can evaluate the progress of a team match by match during their local league schedule, or you can compile an end-of-league summary if you are scouting a prospective opponent for the playoffs. If your team continues to advance beyond your state or sectional championships, you will want to review the full record of the players at every stage of competition.

For example, the large 18 man roster of a Big East adult league men's team amassed the following records in their league and sectional championships before advancing to the USTA national adult division team championships in Tucson. Notice who played singles and who played doubles for the team you are scouting, or if a player has been used both ways. Check to see who had the best win/loss records. Presume that in the playoffs teams will rely upon their strongest players. The record of the roster used in the sectional championships is more definitive than the local league record if a distinction needs to be made about who you might be facing when you play a team.

BIG EAST MEN'S TEAM RECORD

	Local Singles	League Doubles	New England Singles	Section Doubles
Richard B.	0	3-2		
John B.		7-0		2-1
Chris C.		5-0		0-1
Dennis D.	2-1	3-1		2-0
Jerome K.		6-0		2-0
Don L.	2-1		2-0	
William M.	4-3		0-1	
Ralph P.	2-1	0-1	1-0	1-0
Raymond S.		5-0		0-1
Michael T.		3-0		0-1
Spencer T.		5-0		1-1
Brian M.	1-0	5-0		
Robert N.		3-0		
Daniel P.	2-1	1-0		
Charles P.		6-0		0-1
James A.		4-0		1-1
David Y.		5-0		1-1
Marco P.	3-1	3-1		1-1

(The bold players were used in the lineup of the match to be discussed as follows)

When this Big East team played the author's team at nationals, they used **Don L.** on the first court and **Ralph P.** on the second court in the singles matches. Both men had winning singles records in their sectional championship matches. As might be expected, they used their man with the best doubles record, **John B.**, in the first court doubles match. His partner was **Marco P.** who had a good playing record in singles and doubles, but was only used in doubles matches in their sectional playoffs. As might have been expected, given their excellent playing records, their team used **Michael T.** and **Charles P.** on the second doubles court. Their third court doubles team was **William M.** and **Richard B.**, who were only half-way predictable on paper. You can usually estimate a team's lineup with about 75% accuracy.

PREFERRED PROBABLE LINEUP PREDICTIONS:

The purpose of evaluating a team's roster ratings and playing records is to predict who will be in the lineup and where. First, you must judge who are the best players on the team and presume that they will play against you. Using the *Tennis Link* data about match records, look at the lineup a team uses in their opening match of their local league season or in the playoffs. Even better, look at the match record for the team you are scouting for a match when they have played their strongest league opponent. If this team has played the strongest opponent more than once, look at the lineups used on both occasions. This will give you the best estimate of a team's preferred selection of players when they need to win. You should also study the lineup formations the team uses at critical times. Did they use straight or stacked formations, or vary their tactics during their schedule? Sometimes you have to make an educated guess about what to expect, and this is how you do it.

For example, the preliminary scouting report of the West State adult division women's team compiled the following ratings and win/loss record.

West State Women's League Record

	Singles	Doubles	Rating
Deborah S.	3-0	7-0	3.5
Angie C.		7-0	3.0
Kimberly C.	1-0	7-0	3.5
Lisa W.	2-0	5-0	3.5
Katrina P.	3-1	5-0	3.5
Debbie G.	2-1	8-0	3.5
Shauna W.	4-1	3-0	3.5
Mary D.	2-0	5-1	3.5
Donna C.	2-0	7-0	3.0
Sabrina H.	0-1	4-1	3.0

The total record indicates who has the best winning records, but not necessarily who would be used in a crucial match. By reviewing the team's match records in their league, you can identify which were the key matches on their schedule. The West State women's team had won a six-team league with an undefeated 10-0 record after playing each of the other teams twice. Two of their opponents had 7-3 records. In their first encounter with one of these strong rival teams the West State women lineup was as follows:

West State vs. Strong Rival in 1st Match-up

#1 Singles	Shauna W.
#2 Singles	Katrina P.
#1 Doubles	Kimberly C. & Debbie G.
#2 Doubles	Deborah S. & Angie C.
#3 Doubles	Lisa W. & Mary D.

In order to confirm the lineup patterns of the West State women, it was useful to study the lineup they used in their re-match with their same strong rival which was as follows:

San Angelo vs. Strong Rival in 2nd Match-up

#1 Singles	Sabrina H.
#2 Singles	Shauna W.
#1 Doubles	Kimberly C. & Debbie G.
#2 Doubles	Deborah S. & Katrina P.
#3 Doubles	Lisa W. & Donna C.

Comparison of the two lineups shows that the West State team relied upon the same six players in both matches. If you were preparing to play this team, you would plan as if these six women would appear against your team. Your scouting report should also determine how your opponent's key players will likely be deployed when they play you. The next step is to study the individual playing records of their key players to see where they were used in their team's lineups when they have been in league matches. Continuing to use the example of the West State women's team, the first analysis should be made about the use of their singles players.

SINGLES COURT ANALYSIS:

Since one player (**Shauna W.**) was used on both court #1 and court #2 in the matches against their chief rival; initially, it looked like the West State team would employ the **singles switch** formation on occasion. Using the *Tennis Link* data for the individual playing record of a team member, you can determine the most frequent court assignment for any given player. In this example, the singles court playing record for Shauna W. was as follows:

Singles Match Record for Shauna W.

Match #---937 Court #1 - a victory
Match #---941 Court #1 - a loss against the strong rival team
Match #---946 Court #1 - a victory
Match #---956 Court #2 - a victory against the strong rival team
Match #---961 Court #1 - a victory

SINGLES LINEUP CONCLUSIONS:

Shauna W.'s most frequent utilization was in the #1 singles matches. She was switched to the #2 only in match #---956 because she had lost against the same team when she had played them on the #1 court in match #---941. In your scouting report, you would plan as if Shauna would be playing on the #1 court against you unless your team had previously played and beaten her in another match. For the other singles match, the West State team might be expected to use the woman most frequently used in singles matches who would not be identified as crucial to doubles matches. In this example, **Katrina P.** was used in four singles matches in the nine times she was used in team matches. She was nominated as the player most likely to appear in the #2 singles court match. The West State probable preferred singles courts lineup prediction was:

Court #1 – Shauna W.
Court #2 – Katrina P.

DOUBLES COURTS ANALYSIS:

The scouting report analysis of a team's doubles match lineups is morecomplicated because teams often mix-up their partnerships in their team lineups. First you try to determine who have been partners the most often, and then calculate on which courts they have been the most frequently deployed.

Study the *Tennis Link* individual playing records for each key team player who has been used in the doubles matches. In the example of the West State women's team, the four key players of interest had the following records:

Doubles Match Record for Debbie G.
In eight doubles matches, she played with Kimberly C. on five occasions;
        (twice with Katrina P., & once with Lisa W.)
Debbie played on court #1 in six matches, and twice on court #2 in the lineup.

Doubles Match Record for Kimberley C.
In seven doubles matches, she played with Debbie G. on five occasions;
        (once each with Shauna W. & Mary D.)
Kimberley played on court #1 in six matches, and once on court #2 in the lineup.

Doubles Matches Record for Deborah S.
In seven doubles matches, she played with Angie C. three times; with Mary D. twice;
        (once each with Katrina P. & Sabrina H.)
Deborah played on court #1 twice, on court #2 in three matches, and on court #3 twice.

Doubles Match Record for Lisa W.
In five doubles matches, she played with Mary D. twice;
    (once each with Sabrina H., Debbie G. and Donna C.)
Lisa played on court #3 in four matches and once on court #1 in the lineup.

DOUBLES LINEUP CONCLUSIONS:

The West State team was exceptionally strong in their doubles lineup, having won 29 out of 30 league doubles matches during their regular season. Their team tended to put their best doubles players (Debbie. G. & Kimberly C.) on the first court in their key matches. Their team had good depth in the second and third court doubles matches, so their team was expected to use a straight doubles format. The probable preferred doubles lineup prediction was:

> Court #1 - Debbie G. & Kimberly C.
> Court #2 - Deborah S. & Angie C.
> Court #3 -.Lisa W. & Mary D.

LINEUP SCOUTING RECOMMENDATIONS:

The West State team record was impressive, having had won 46 out of the 50 courts played in their league matches. Their losses occurred three times in singles and only once in doubles. The best lineup strategy was to try to steal a win on the second singles court lineup by using a **singles switch (2-1)** formation. In the doubles matches, since the West State team put their best players on court #1, the **downward slide (3-1-2)** formation would help overcome their strength and depth in that part of the lineup. The prediction was that a team victory would likely depend upon the outcome of the second and third doubles court matches that could be expected to be decided by match ending tiebreakers.

MATCH RESULTS:

In their opening playoff match with a weaker Coastal City team, The West State women won 4-1 by using most of the predicted probable preferred lineup. The results were as follows:

> Singles court #1   - Shauna W. (won)
> Singles court #2   - Katrina P. (lost)
> Doubles court #1 - Debbie G. & Kimberly C. (won)
> Doubles court #2 - Deborah S. & Mary D. (won)
> Doubles court #3 - Lisa W. & Donna C. (won)

In their second playoff match, the West State women played a strong East State team. The East State team prepared for the West State team by using the recommended scouting report match lineup strategies. The lineup projections for this match were less certain since the West State team was expected to vary their lineup in order to use other players from their roster in the playoffs. The East State team was able to win one of the singles courts despite an unexpected singles switch in the West State lineup. As had been foretold, the contest was decided by the second and third court doubles matches that both ended in tiebreakers. Each team won one of the tiebreakers; but as expected, the West State won on the first court doubles court to give them the team victory by 3-2 in court wins. The West State women used the following lineup against the East State team:

Singles court #1 – Mary D. (lost)
Singles court #2 - Shauna W. (won)

Doubles court #1 – Debbie G. & Kimberly C. (won)
Doubles court #2 - Angie C. & Donna C. (won in tie-breaker)
Doubles court #3 - Deborah S. & Sabrina H. (lost in tie-breaker)

West State went on to win their third match in their four-team playoff flight, and advanced to the semi-finals of the sectional championships.

SCOUTING REMINDERS:

Remember that the other teams are capable of scouting your lineup patterns and should be presumed to have prepared for you in the same way you try to prepare for them. You will have to spend some time summarizing the lineup formations you have used to determine how predictable your team might appear to others. Consequently, you will occasionally have to set up your opponents by varying your personnel utilization before the BIG matches. When possible, use other formations in the matches preceding the time you play your chief rival. Big Brother is watching you.

Keep in mind that lineup adjustments are occasionally made after both teams have arrived for the pre-match warm-up period. In order to disguise the actual lineup, you will be using, you might have some of your extra players participate in the team warm-up periods so the other team can't be completely sure of who will be in the matches. The extra players are a good precaution to have game ready substitutes in case of unexpected team injuries or illness. Since most lineups include three doubles matches, it would help to have an extra doubles team during practice to provide two full courts of doubles as a training aid during the warm-up period. Try to let your singles players practice separately on their own court, and rotate the backup singles on the roster into that part of the team warm-up too.

After you analyze and study about another team and their players, try to make informed choices about what your team should do when you play each other. Your teammates may have background information about your opponent that will help fill in the blanks. Sometimes you can exchange information with other league teams who can supply you with helpful hints about what to expect. After you have reached your conclusions about your opponents, wait 24 hours before committing yourself to a plan of action. Give your intuition time to process all your considerations, and then go for it. Sometimes you will guess right, and other times you will get an unexpected surprise. It's all part of the game, and keeps things interesting.

Make a written estimate of what you expect the other team will do and compose your team's prospective lineup to use against them. The author sends copies of his report to all of his team members so they will feel well-informed about their upcoming match. The advance notice gives his team a chance to critique the scouting report before the match in case there is a better course of action than the one the captain has proposed. However, some team captains prefer to make limited use of their scouting report to keep some of their players from getting anxious about how good their prospective opponent might be. Take a copy of your scouting report to the match and compare your projections with the actual lineup used against you. Pay attention to your opponent's doubles partnerships to identify whether one player in each tandem is noticeably stronger than the other. If so, notify your doubles team about the weaker player so an effective attack plan on that player can be formulated.

A scouting report is only a piece of paper. Your best estimates will only be 75% accurate, and the other teams will be doing their best to thwart your plans anyway.
Pre-match deliberations and preparations usually increase your chances of winning, and can be the difference maker in closely competitive situations. In the final analysis, all matches have to be won on the courts with racquets and balls, not by pencil engineering. We still have to play our way to victory even with a good game plan. May your strokes be as good as your intentions.

Chapter 5   WINNING TIEBREAKERS

If you study the match scores between contending teams in local leagues, and the scores of USTA sectional and national championship matches, you will see that most of these important contests were determined by tiebreakers. If you analyze a team's final league or playoff standings, the team's record can virtually be summarized in terms of how many tiebreakers the team played and won during the schedule. The author's team has been involved in several league and sectional championship matches where every court ended in a tiebreaker. Literally, the title was decided by the bounce of the ball more than just once. As a consequence, winning teams must concentrate on how to master these all-important playing situations. Many players consider the fortunes of playing tiebreakers to be like rolling dice or buying a lottery ticket – your number might come up, or it might not. For sure, the stakes are high; and if you win, you really feel like celebrating. But if you lose, the agony of defeat seems all the worse from having come so close to victory and being denied the win. In those disconsolate moments, tiebreakers truly become heartbreakers. Fortunately, there are things a team can do that will increase the chances of winning when it matters the most. A winning team will practice tiebreakers every time they go to the courts to play tennis so they can get it right when it really counts.

One adage about match-ending tiebreakers is that playing in one is like being caught in an ambush. The military says that the best defense against an ambush is not to get caught in one. Good advance preparation and lineup scouting can help minimize the number of situations where you must rely upon the outcome of tiebreakers to settle your scores. Straight set victories are the only alternative solution for not playing a tiebreaker. Stress to your team the importance of a good start in their matches, and how important it is to win the first set. If you have some players who play better the longer their match continues (or who are late starters), have them play some hard practice games shortly before they begin their team matches. If you do win the first set, then ask yourself, "Do I really want to risk letting this match end in a tiebreaker?" Let the first set victory motivate you to concentrate even more on closing out the match by winning the second set, too. That's how you avoid the tiebreaker ambush in tennis.

Since the best laid plans of mice and men oft times go astray, you will not always win the first set of your matches. In those instances, when you have lost the first set, the use of tiebreakers in lieu of a full third set will allow you to concentrate on making a comeback in the second set. The prospect of a tiebreaker allows the player who is behind in the match to exert their full energy on the remaining games of the contest. You don't have to save energy for later and can let "it" all hang out, leaving "everything" on the court. These are the times when you can make playing tiebreakers work to your advantage. A lot depends upon whether you are the kind of player who never gives up and can come from behind without getting discouraged if you have lost a set already. One way to help players develop such an attitude is to hold practice matches where the players flip a coin to decide who starts out the match with a one-set scoring advantage before play begins. The players who start out behind with the one-set handicap must win the practice set in order to get to a tiebreaker. Of course, winning the set in such a match is no guarantee about what will happen next.

If you become involved in a match-ending tiebreaker, be aware that there is no such thing as match momentum in this situation. Winning either the first or second set does not predict who will win the tiebreaker. Look over your match scoring patterns and you will see that there is no clear indicator within the set scores that will show who will win the tiebreaker. The tiebreaker is truly a complete starting over process in the match. You can forget what has already happened. At this point the match can go either way. Relax and focus; then settle down for the points to come.

Scoring in a tiebreaker makes clearly evident that point runs occur constantly on the court, but are disguised in the archaic scoring system used for standard tennis point keeping. In the normal course of play, contestants frequently win or lose several points in succession. The two-point margin for ending a game requires that someone have a point run to finish playing each game. Game scores of 40-love are common, illustrating how tennis points can be won in bunches. Yet in a tiebreaker, winning three points in a row has a different effect than it has in the scoring of an ordinary game in a set. Tiebreaker points are cumulative and not sub-divided into four-point games. Traditional scoring can produce the anomaly of winning a set without having won the most total points in the total games played. Within a set, tie-score games of 40-40 are commonly decided by the advantage point scoring system. In this situation, players frequently win a point, then lose a point and revert back to a deuce tie score. Games may have multiple deuces before someone gains a two point advantage to end the scoring and win the game. Occasional games might be played this closely, but the whole match rarely proceeds with players winning alternating points throughout the contest. That pattern becomes quite evident in a tiebreaker.

Tiebreakers play differently because of the change in the cumulative point scoring system, and the rapid two-point rotation of taking turns serving the ball among the players. Keeping the score continuously close or even is urgently important because a point run can be so decisive in this crucial situation. In a tiebreaker, you must concentrate on every point as if you were already at the add-in or add-out of an ordinary game in a set. Losing one point, then winning the next point is acceptable in the course of a tiebreaker. You must never lose two successive points without immediately winning the next two points in a row. The slightest deviation from this point winning pattern will result in an eventual defeat. The progress in tiebreakers can be measured by the "mini-breaks" within the two-point increments of the scoring at any point in the tiebreaker. Focus on the score in two-point intervals and you will pace yourself better in a tiebreaker.

As soon as someone scores five points in a match-ending tiebreaker, it becomes crunch time. Even though the score is only at the mid-point of the ten-point finish, the end of the match is about to begin. To stay alert and focused, you might think of the tiebreaker as being the equivalent of two regular games in length. After winning five points, someone has finished the so-called "first game," and there is only one game left before someone will become the match victor. You must win this last game to claim the tiebreaker. When someone calls out that their score is five points, that should be your cue to start sprinting to the finish or else you will be left behind.

Closing out a tiebreaker is hard work and a real danger point in the match. When a player has won eight points in a ten-point tiebreaker, the end seems near - but is yet still far away. You can stall at the very time you feel that victory is within your grasp. That is because the dynamic of the scoring system is played in two-point increments throughout the tiebreaker, at the end just like in the beginning. Winning the last two points can be as difficult as losing the last five pounds on a weight loss diet. The other team will become more intense than ever on stopping you from winning by the necessary two point margin to end the match. The score can shift back and forth, giving you the impression that the match is slipping away. More than ever, you must concentrate on playing the ball without regard to what is the score. As soon as someone has scored eight points, that is the time you need to take a deep breath and relax before finishing your next point. Eight should be the cue to think only about the bounce of the ball and the swing of your racquet. Focusing on the playing process will give you the results you are seeking anytime you play tennis.

In tiebreakers, players will sometimes force their hits trying to end the point because they have gotten excited by the prospect of winning soon. Likewise, some players become cautious and tentative in their play to avoid making mistakes so they won't lose at the end of a match. Advise everyone that during a tiebreaker, more than ever, just to watch the ball and to stay in the moment instead of wondering about what is going to happen next. Nevertheless, there are some players who choke in tight situations. There are others who thrive in clutch situations. A team should keep track of the tiebreaking win/loss record for each player. If there is a noticeable pattern for someone, then that might become an important consideration for choosing who plays in the lineup at crucial times when you can inevitably expect to be involved in tiebreakers. Put your money players in the court match-ups at the times and places where you know there are going to be close contests.

During match-ending tiebreakers, remember that you are starting the equivalent of a regular third set. Thus, in a doubles match you have the usual option of choosing who should serve first for your team. In a tiebreaker, determine whether one player serves better into the sun or against the wind if these have been factors in the match thus far. The Coman tiebreak procedure has replaced the six-point changeover rule where each doubles partners used to end up serving from both ends of the courts. This has been a change for the better in the changeover routines since you will always serve from the same end of the court throughout the tiebreaker, just like in a regulation set. As always, have the player who has been the most successful carrying their serve go first for your team. Likewise, you have the option of choosing who will receive the opponent's service on which court. You will usually want to stay in the same receiving alignment you have been using in the match because it was good enough to win one set for you. As for the playing of the subsequent points, in the words of the immortal football coach Darrell Royal, "Dance with the one who brung you." Stick to your strengths and what has been working for you. Even then, the outcome may still feel like it depends upon who gets the breaks.

Tiebreakers can be lifesavers in very hot weather, especially for senior and super-senior divisions. Players, on the other hand, often conclude that while tiebreakers produce a match winner, they do not necessarily determine who has the better team. If you win a tiebreaker, adopt the attitude that you have just dodged a bullet rather than gloat about some great achievement. When you lose a tiebreaker, don't catastrophize the results. Win some, lose some, and hope it will even out over time in other matches to come. May your number come up often in the tennis lottery of life.

Chapter 6

THE PLAYOFFS

PRE-TOURNAMENT PREPARATIONS:

After your planning and training have produced a winning team and you have become the league champions, it is time to compete at the next level of tennis. Playing in a state, sectional, or national championship tournament requires as much preparation as it does to organize a team before the start of a local league schedule.

Getting everyone on board for the playoffs is a big task. At the earliest possible time, the team members should be told when and where the championships are to be played. The team captain must insure that there will be enough players to meet the minimum number of players required to participate in the championship (enough for one full lineup for the matches) before submitting a roster of eligible players to the tournament director. There might be a team entry fee expense that will have to be prorated among those players who commit for the playoffs.

Unless your town is hosting the big event, your team will almost certainly have to make travel plans to attend the tournament. This requires some concentrated planning and coordination of transportation and lodging arrangements on the road. Some tournament sites are more accessible than others. One of the best USTA national championships destinations is Tucson, Arizona, for ease of arrival and use of centralized court facilities. Conversely, air flights directly into Palm Springs, California, fill up quickly and you might have to land at Ontario or Los Angeles. The Palm Springs tournament uses multiple small nine-court playing sites that may require shuttling your team from one court site to another during the course of your tournament match schedule. Wherever you play, allow some time for site seeing, because your trip can also be a vacation.

Despite its importance, not everyone on the team may be available to make the trip. Some people might not be able to afford the extra expenses, especially if air travel must be used. If your team is playing in a national championship, you might be given some travel grant money by your USTA sectional office. Publicity about a local sports team can be valuable advertising for a community; so approach your local chamber of commerce about getting local sponsors to underwrite your team expenses. After the tournament, publicly acknowledge any sponsorships and assistance your team received, preferably in the local media.

Most championship sites will have a host headquarters hotel where teams can make reservations at a discount from the standard hotel room rate. The tournament room quota usually fills up early, so the sooner the team can make reservations the better. If your players need to economize on their lodging expense, by all means do some comparison shopping on the internet or over the phone. Sharing rooms and provision of local ground transportation becomes part of the advance planning. It may not be feasible for everyone to stay at the same motel. In which case, the players must know how and where to find each other when they are out of town. Exchange cell phone numbers with each other for ease of communications. Each player needs an advance printed copy of the tournament match schedule, the court locations, and have early notice about their prospective utilization in the lineups. Most playoffs will guarantee a team at least a minimum three match schedule in the event. Lineups should be made that will assure each player participates in at least two matches; given the time and money it takes for each person to be there.

As part of the advance reservations procedures, many tournaments will schedule a social event for all players. If there is a planned dinner, then the team captain will have to collect money from each player who wants a meal ticket and send the tournament director a check for the total ticket order. The dinner tickets will be issued to the team captain during pre-tournament registration. Tournaments are like a tennis convention where the off-court interactions are one of the most enjoyable parts of the playing experience; so smooze as much as possible while you are there.

After arriving for the playoffs, the team captains must register their teams with the tournament director and pick up their playoffs materials. Most big events give a tournament T-shirt to each player. When you pick up the team's bundle of T-shirts, give the site coordinators a written list of the shirt sizes needed to outfit your team members. At USTA sectional and national tournaments, the team captain will be given a tennis accessory as a present and reward for the work have done to bring the team to the playoffs. Before competition begins, there will be a team captains' meeting to make introductions, discuss the playing schedule, interpret rulings, and answer questions about the tournament. The tournament director will ask each team for a cell phone contact number, which will become an important communications link if the tournament has weather delays and changes have to made in the match schedules.

At championship matches the team lineups must be given to the scorekeeper at least 30 minutes before the scheduled match time. No changes may be made in the lineup after the names have been submitted to the tournament director's desk, except for emergency illnesses or injuries. **No one's name should be written on the official lineup roster unless the person is physically present at the courts and has been personally seen by the team captain before the entry deadline.** Team members should expect to arrive at their match site about one hour before play is to begin. The team captain must insure there will be no forfeits due to unexpected absences or late arrivals for the match time.

Prior to the match starting time, the players must be available to come immediately to the tournament desk when the director announces that a court is available for their part of the contest. Typically, you can expect a staggered start and finish of your lineup's matches. The tournament director will assign matches on a court-by-court basis as playing places become open at your tennis site. In some instances, the director will ask the contestants to identify themselves at the desk before being given permission to begin play. If courts become available before the stated starting times, teams can be asked to begin playing matches earlier than expected. Everyone must be ready to play on short notice. Likewise, if the tournament matches run behind schedule, the teams must wait patiently near the director's table and go to the courts as soon as they become available to prevent adding further delay to the day's playing schedule.

After a match is completed, all players must return to the scorekeeper's desk to report and to confirm the scores. When each court score has been recorded for the full match, the team captain must sign the score sheet to verify the results. Before the team leaves the tennis site, the players should be reminded about when and where their next matches will be played.

GIFT EXCHANGES AT MATCH TIME:

At the national championships, as a gesture of goodwill toward each other, many teams exchange gifts before the start of their match. Have each player in your lineup hand a keepsake present to the person they will be playing. Products from your home town or state of residence will be delightful topics of conversation later when you see each other at the tournament. Your team will end up with a nice collection of souvenirs you can show off when you get back home.

PLAYOFF MATCH STRATEGIES:

Championship tournaments are like playing an end of season college football bowl game because of the delays between winning your local league and playing for the state or national titles. The gaps in team activity can be months long, making it difficult to sustain the intensity and momentum achieved while qualifying for the playoffs. When possible during the waiting period before the playoff dates, the team members should continue to enter competitive events in other tennis leagues programs or tournaments. Sometime during the month preceding the playoff matches, have a team meeting and practice to restore a sense of identity and to revive enthusiasm for the coming event.

One way to reassure your teammates about their suitability to play for the championships is to re-enact a motivating scene from the great sports movie **"Hoosiers."** In this true story, the little basketball team from Hickory, Indiana, was escorted onto the big city gymnasium floor before playing for the state championships. The coach had a player measure the height to the basket rim from the floor to insure that the distance was still only ten feet tall, just like back home in their school gym. Remind your team that the tennis court where you are going is still only 78 feet long, and that the net will be only 36 inches high at the center cord, just like always. Don't let the players become awed by their circumstances, or content with the status of merely being there. Your team hasn't come to just gain good experience; you have come to win, and win you most certainly can.

Reassure your team and motivate them with the knowledge that your playoff opponents will not necessarily be stronger than the contending teams you have already faced in your local league. However, every match will feel like you are fighting to win your hardest regular season match. Remember how you won those tough matches and then do it again. **You may be sure that in the championships your matches will be so close that they will all likely be decided by tiebreakers.** Prepare accordingly.

Plan your lineup strategies to win the opening playoff match at all costs to give your team confidence for the rest of the tournament. Plan to make your substitutions in the later matches. If possible, the team captain should try to observe the first match to evaluate the performance of the team and scout other matches. After the first match is finished, the captain will be more relaxed and better able to focus on their own playing skills when it is their turn in the lineup. No matter who is in the lineup, have full confidence in them because they will need it. Watch for which players have the "hot racquets" and use them frequently. Capitalize upon those players who are winning because success breeds success.

Things happen fast during a tournament and you must monitor the progress of events as they rapidly unfold. Follow the tournament match results of your competitors closely. Ask the scorekeeper to let you look at the score sheets and write down the lineups being used by your rivals and their match scores. Check your scouting reports to see if the other teams have brought their full rosters or if they have notable absences. In a four team flight, you can lose one contest and still have hopes of winning your group's competition. If your team loses twice and are effectively out of contention for the championship, your team can still affect what will be the final team standings. **Be advised that the USTA can levy sanctions against any team that fails to complete all of their matches at a sectional or national championship tournament.** Stay and play because any victory will be good for team morale. Sometimes when the pressure of winning the championship has been lifted from your expectations, your team can relax and enjoy their remaining matches as a recreation opportunity to have fun playing the game we all love and make friends with the people you will meet. Good luck when your team is on top. Win or lose, the memories of those precious times will last you a lifetime.

Chapter 7
ESPRIT DE CORPS AND MORALE

The most enjoyable and important components of team tennis are the camaraderie and esprit de corps that can develop among teammates. Banding together for the common objective of winning a league championship can be a rich bonding experience that leads to true and lasting friendships. One hallmark of esprit de corps is the lively banter that takes place with each other before, during, and after a match. Giving encouragements, congratulations, and consolations to teammates builds up team morale and contributes to good performance on the courts. Here are a few examples of what you might say on game day at various times of the match.

REMARKS BEFORE A MATCH:

Try to lessen the pre-match tensions about winning or losing. The more important the match is, the more you want to minimize the drama of the situation. You might say, "It's only a game, (not life or death)," or "they can beat you, but they can't eat you," or "whatever happens, we'll still love you." Express profound, exaggerated confidence in your teammate's ability to win in a good natured manner. Jokingly tell them that the other team wants to get their autograph, and have their pictures taken with them. Keep things light and loose without being frivolous, and affirm that your teammates need only to play their game and the rest will take care of itself.

Sometimes team members will discuss the different ways that other players may try to psych out someone before a match. To counter any mental advantage an opponent might try to gain over a junior's tennis team, one imaginative captain and coach composed a list of whimsical one-liners for the amusement and confidence building of the girls in the team's lineup. The following gags are some examples of the comic material that can be used as a constructive diversion for nervous competitors before a match.

~ Mention to your opponent you were born in a foreign country and came to live in America at the Nick Bollettieri Tennis Academy in Florida. Claim that Maria Sharapova was your roommate, and that both of you have worked hard not to have an accent.

~Tell your opponent that where you come from the winner gets to keep the loser's racquet as a trophy, but that your travel bag is too full to add more to it - so you would rather just play for fun today.

~Ask the other girls if you can hurry and get started so you won't be late for your photographer's picture taking session for the new Girls of Tennis Calendar.

~Mention that you need to find a bank that will cash the check you got from Wimbledon.

~Finally, complain that someone must have given your unlisted phone number to Andy Roddick, because he just won't stop calling you.

WORDS WHILE WATCHING A MATCH:

The most sensitive time for communications is during the play of a match. If you are on the sidelines watching a teammate play, try not to distract them with interactions that will make them self-conscious about how they are playing. Help your team keep their focus on the ball, not on their surroundings. Politely applaud well played points as tennis etiquette permits because it can stimulate and positively reinforce your teammate's high level of performance on the court. If you can't tell what the score is, wait until a changeover and quietly ask about the status of their match. Keep in mind that by inquiring about the score, your teammates may feel embarrassed if they are behind at the time you have asked. So be discrete and hesitant to interrupt the flow of the game with conversation. **If your players should ask you about the progress of your team on the other courts, keep in mind that giving out scores in other matches can be construed as violating the USTA rules against coaching from the sidelines.** Just politely say that you don't know or that everyone is doing their best.

If you are in a doubles match, there are some very pertinent things you can and can't say in the midst of the play. First, you must find out if your partner is internal or external in their personal orientation. Before the match, ask if they need a quiet relationship so they can maintain their inner focus on how they are playing. In which case, contain your conversation to remarks between games and during changeover rest periods. If your partner responds to spontaneous responses on the court, then keep everything positive and forgiving. You may say anything you want about what you notice the opponents are doing in the match, to include what will work against them. These remarks can be very helpful if they are in the form of a scouting report. On the other hand, don't try to improve your partner's strokes by coaching them about how to hit the ball better during the course of a match. You can seriously hurt their game and frustrate a player by what will always be interpreted as a personal criticism in the heat of battle. Doubles partnerships have been known to break up because one person was trying to be too helpful when the other person was struggling with their game.

COMMENTARY AFTER THE MATCH:

Players usually exchange pleasantries with each other on the court at the end of a match. Assure your partner that you have enjoyed playing with them whether you really have or not. If you have won the match, celebrate; but not too excessively in front of your opponents. Give your partner credit for their part in the victory no matter how much or how little they have contributed to the final score. You might even say things like, "Thanks partner, you carried me." The elation of the moment will generate a lot of goodwill, because it is well-known in sports that "Winning Cures Cancer." Even then, some partners will be self-critical about how they could have played better. Remind them that "a win is a win," no matter how ugly the match was played.

One of the most important times to say the right thing to a player is after they have lost a match. **Remember that for most players it doesn't matter if you win or lose, until you lose.** Consolation and support is always appreciated. Sympathize first and then gradually transcend your remarks to hope for the future. Even though some of these remarks sound like clichés, the word will be greatly appreciated if you can say them with sincerity.

"You may have been outscored, but you were never beaten. You just ran out of time."

"It's a scientific fact that exactly half of all people who play tennis, lose."

"The ball bounced the wrong way this time."

"I'm sorry we lost, but you could take them in a rematch."

"You played well and deserved to have more to show for your efforts."

"You were just protecting your playing ratings to keep from getting promoted to higher level next year."

"If we replay this match over some food and drinks, we might discover that you actually won and didn't know it."

You might borrow a line from a scene in the classic movie **"Little Big Man"** when the Indian chief thought it was time to lie down and join the Great Spirit, but didn't die. When he awoke, he said, "Sometimes the magic doesn't work." Amen

TEAM BUILDING ACTIVITES:

Team members have excellent opportunities to socialize and interact by traveling together on the way to and from matches. Car pooling to the courts allows players a chance to talk about their work and families, in addition to providing cost saving transportation – especially on out-of-town trips. The time and effort it takes to arrange coordinated team movement will help bring the players closer together and thereby boost morale.

As time permits immediately after a league match, invite the team to enjoy some refreshments together. You might even include the players from the other team in the convivialities. Bring snacks and sodas to the courts if there is no concessionaire at the playing site. Some teams take the time to go to a local restaurant to extend their fellowship around a table together. You might refer to eating Mexican food as your nacho therapy. Sometimes team members congratulate or console each other by buying a round of drinks, or even paying for the meal. At the end of the league schedule, players especially enjoy meeting and eating at someone's home to reminisce about the team's record and make plans for entering more league programs. You can measure the cohesiveness of a team by how much time they are willing to spend with each other after matches to replay their victories or defeats.

FAMILY AND FANS:

Be sure to include your family members and friends in your team's activities. Bring portable chairs and sun umbrellas for their seating comfort when they come to watch your matches. Help your fans get acquainted with each other so they can become your official cheering section. Give them matching shirts to wear on the sidelines. Salute their partisan role in urging you onward to victory with table toasts at refreshment time. Take lots of pictures and make keepsake copies for everyone. These photos can be sued for after match publicity. During their three appearances at the USTA 2005 nationals, the author's team and supporters wore spiral tie-dye rainbow colored shirts. Their group picture was shown on the USTA website as a tournament highlight. That kind of recognition really helps a team's morale and can be obtained by any set of prayers willing to use some imagination and promotional efforts.

Chapter 8
THE FINAL WORD - SPORTSMANSHIP

The motto of good sportsmanship clearly stipulates that what matters most at the end of a career is how we have played the game. Attitude and character are what endure long after our records have been eclipsed by others. Tennis players must learn to be gracious losers and magnanimous winners.

Be sure to congratulate whoever wins your league and praise them as being good representatives from your area or district. Encourage them to do well when they advance to the playoffs. Your losses to them will look better on your record if it took a champion to beat you.

If your team should become the league champion, let your closest contender know that you are going to recommend their team to the sectional and district coordinators for inclusions in the playoffs as a wild card entry in the championships. Assure your fellow competitors that your team thinks their team is good enough to win in the state playoffs, too; and that you would like for them to join you in a sweep to the finals together.

The more goodwill you generate, the better league play will be for your team thereafter. Avoid bitter rivalries because they only motivate opponents to strive against you more determinedly. For after all, what does it profit a person to conquer the world if they lose their soul?

Live and let live, and may your years be long upon this earth with your first serve always an ace.

Shalom and Amen.

ABOUT THE AUTHOR

Sam Hopkins was born in a San Antonio, Texas, which is a tennis town; but he didn't realize that until after he had graduated from Edison High School. Upon enrolling in Trinity University, he cheered for the great tennis teams coached by the legendary Clarence Mabry. The eventual Wimbledon men's single champion, Chuck McKinley, played for the Trinity Tigers in those far gone days. Sam was inspired to learn how to keep score and hit a ball so he could follow the school's team more closely. After college graduation, he and a fellow tennis-loving Trinity buddy enrolled in the Perkins School of Theology at Southern Methodist University. After classes, the two hackers smacked an old fashioned white tennis balls on a city court until the balls were black with dirt and barely bounced any more. Thus, the love of his favorite sport was hewn and fashioned.

In order to pursue his playing interests after graduation from SMU, Sam frequently organized tennis tournaments in the towns and cities where he lived. He rarely won any trophies or titles for twenty years. In this period, after coming back home from the Vietnam War, he used the G.I. Bill to earn a doctoral degree in counseling psychology at the University of Texas at Austin. Even while working in a full time job, pursuing strenuous graduate studies, and supporting a wife and three children, Sam found time to enter intramural tennis tournaments with a classmate who was to become a lifelong men's doubles partner. Sam's mental health career brought him to East Texas, where he founded the Jacksonville (TX) Tennis Association. Among the first programs he instituted was a local team tennis league, a program format well suited to his gregarious nature and organizing abilities. This expertise in team tennis led to statewide tennis league renown for Jacksonville later in his playing career.

Sam is the proudest of the tennis successes his family has achieved. His wife, Patsy, played for senior women and super senior women's teams that won championships for many years before Sam ever made the playoffs. Their oldest daughter, Jeannie, won a tennis scholarship at East Texas State University where her team advanced to the national championships for four years. Her younger sister, Christine, was an equally strong high school team tennis player. Grandson, Kyle, won his high school mixed doubles district championship; and granddaughter, Sarah, won the district doubles title and a third place regional medal for her high school. On one occasion, three generations of the family's females all won medals together in the same tournament. What more could any man ask?

www.ingramcontent.com/pod-product-compliance
Lightning Source LLC
Chambersburg PA
CBHW061457040426
42450CB00008B/1389